LMNTRE
POEMS

Published by Tŷ Llên

First published 1999 by
Tŷ Llen publications
Tŷ Llen
Swansea

ISBN

Acknowledments are due to the Glynn Vivian and the Watkins family for
permission to reproduce the drawing of Vernon Watkins by Alfred Janes on the
back cover and to David Perry for the use of the photograph of Alan Perry.

All royalties from the sale of this book will go to further the work of
the Cyrenians Cymru Arts Scheme.

Printed and bound in Great Britain by
Brynymor Press, Llandarcy.

This book is published by Tŷ Llên Publications at The Dylan Thomas Centre,
Somerset Place, Swansea. Other publications are:
* 'Who Killed Dylan Thomas' by Adrian Mitchell
  illustrated by Ralph Steadman
* 'The Dylan Thomas Trail'
  (1) Swansea City Centre
  for a full details of these and future publications contact:
  Tel:01792 463980
  Fax: 01792 463993
  E-mail: dylan,thomas@cableol.co.uk
  Website: http://www.dylanthomas.org

CITY AND COUNTY OF SWANSEA • DINAS A SIR ABERTAWE

Contents

Foreword

One facet of Vernon Watkins' personality seems to have been neglected by, or unknown to his reviewers and obituarists. His readers know the poet who believed that all lyrical poetry should be exalted, to whom 'art is the principle of all creation'; but only his family and friends – and of course his wartime colleagues – knew the man who delighted in every aspect of the comic, from the most robust to the most subtle.

It was not only their interest in poetry that made his friendship with Dylan Thomas so close; it was their relish for every comic incident in life or literature. Their own lives were full of comedy, as though they had been two Welsh Marx brothers, since neither could even faintly pretend to cope with the practical necessities of life. But because the tools of their trade were words, they took an especial delight in every kind of comic verse and prose; Carroll, Lear, Harry Graham's **Ruthless Rhymes,** Belloc's epigrams, Logan Pearsall Smith's **Trivia**. Vernon, who never bought a newspaper except for the cricket scores, would buy the old News Chronicle every day to read his beloved D.B. Wyndham Lewis's column as Timothy Shy; Dylan, who read every newspaper, would keep Vernon in touch with his beloved Beachcomber from the Daily Express. On Saturdays, when Vernon cycled to Laugharne, his first question would be:
    "What was the best bit of Beachcomber this week?"

"Oh, I think I liked the Roman matron interviewing a sentry on Hadrian's wall:
'Are you Appius Claudius?' 'No, mum, I'm as miserable as 'ell.'
Or the hunting rhyme:
'See how defenceless and unarmed they go
To meet the onset of the deadly foe,
Protected only by the loyal pack
Against the fox's terrible attack.'"

"That's very good. And did you see Timothy Shy's
'Hark! A hubbub at the Zoo!

Uncle George has fallen through!
Twenty stone of beef and blare...
Pressure has been brought to Bear.'"

"Oh, yes; why don't we write poems like that?"

In fact they did compose a great deal of comic verse, hardly any of it, unfortunately, on paper. As a relaxation from the strain of composition, they would revise Palgrave's Golden Treasury:

It was a summer evening / Old Kafka's work was done
or *Nobbly, nobbly, Cape St. Vincent*
or *The holy time is quiet as a bun.*

When Dylan's son Llewellyn was born, Vernon wrote several poems for him, including the backwards-and-forwards acrostic printed here. His own five children were a continual source of delight and inspiration to him; their fresh and innovative use of language amused him but was also a gold-mine from which he quarried nuggets for his own verse. When his two eldest children began to read, he was brought into contact with a kind of literature new to him, the world of books for small children. Some met with his approval; others appalled him. He commented on them in verse, often neatly printed on the fly-leaf. His daughter, a passionate admirer in her fifth and sixth year of the Milly-Molly-Mandy books, was enraged to see, as well as a birthday inscription, the verse

Milly-Molly-Mandy / Her legs were very bandy
And when the left leg let her down
She found the right one handy.

Enid Blyton's **Book of Fairies,** containing many vapid poems on gnomes and elves, received the comment

I'd like to state my view of you
In language quite unstinted.

But when I sent it to the press
The printer wouldn't print it.

He was exasperated by the poor quality of much verse for children. Once driven almost to distraction by the failure of rhyme and metre in one of the Rupert Bear books he rewrote every quatrain. Does that book still survive I wonder?

His second son began a memoir of his father, unfinished because of Tristan's early death. He refers often to his father's

'delicate, somewhat arbitrary humour and his relish for puns of appalling banality, which he would often deliver, to the concerted groans of the family, at the Sunday lunch. Or when he went down to the beach below the house, he would say warningly, pointing to my youngest brother, not yet one year old, "Hush! Don't wake the BAY-BEE", conjuring up the vision of some strange insect of enormous magnitude lurking in the crevices of the rocks.

'At another time, when I was studying Old Testament history, he related a story of two families invited to supper with a certain A. The head of one family, arriving at A's door to find the other family already there, remarked genially, "Oh!, I see that A-has-you-ere-us." The more convoluted the story the worse the final pun. When I was reading the Lord of the Rings to him in the evenings, he would challenge me to improvise sentences incorporating the names of characters, as, for example, "Where's my Ara-gorn? Boromir another."; or, "There's a Sauron my Leg-olas." When I was puzzling over my Geometry homework he presented me with the solemn formula, "There are more things in Heaven and Earth, Pi-ratio, than are dreamt of in your philosophy."

'On winter mornings, he would appear in the living-room, adjust his tie before the mirror over the mantelpiece and chant an incantation which never varied, "Grabachi, Grambani, Bolinoko, Busoni, Phaldiron the plumed hero, and, coming in last, …back from his long travels" (a prolonged pause) "the Pra!" We children, impatient for the next part of the programme, grew to hate the old Pra; because my father would then solemnly stand on his chair, take a heaped spoonful of Golden Syrup in his right hand, and drop the golden stream unerringly on to his porridge. We waited with a mixture of horror and fascination for the rare occasions on which the experiment was unsuccessful.

'While travelling to Swansea on the bus, he and I collaborated in an immensely complicated serial story concerning mainly the court of Wunce, the capital of Terengaria, and the antics of its King and Queen, Louis and Raspberry, and their generals, Babble, Confucian and Glumm. When one day I tried to unravel the possible interpretations psychiatrists might deduce from these goings-on, my father replied in the celebrated words of the King of Hearts, "If there's no meaning in it, that saves a world of trouble, you know, as we needn't try to find any."'

It was a habit of Vernon's to interpolate comic or fantastic material among otherwise serious remarks, and to do it with a solemn face. He ended his maiden speech as a newly-elected Fellow of the Royal Society of Literature by saying, "We of this Society should remember the closing words of the Eskimo delegate to the last P.E.N. conference: "Littakuk gugnuk Frottakuk! – Literature knows no frontiers.'" These stirring words were, of course, the sole invention of Timothy Shy, but the audience of intellectuals applauded decorously, and no fugitive smile was seen.

On another occasion, at the opening of an exhibition by the 56 Group at the Glynn Vivian Gallery in Swansea, it only gradually dawned on the distinguished audience that Vernon's speech contained a hideous, though partially concealed, pun on the name of every exhibitor. At first there was the occasional furtive smile, then a few giggles, and at last a storm of laughter. But Vernon maintained throughout the serious and concerned expression of an art critic.

We have omitted from this book poems that seemed too closely linked to the occasion for which they were written, except for a long poem written for a Literary Society in Cornwall of which Charles Causley was Chairman. The poems we have included show the range and versatility of Vernon's light and occasional verse. The two short poems for his elder children are included because they are acrostics, as is the immensely accomplished acrostic for his godson Llewellyn Thomas, of which both first and last letters of every line spell the child's name. The acrostics on the name of Auden and Lowell were written very rapidly in response to a challenge from Dr. Daniel Jones. **Pooly, Drippy, People** was composed for his second son, who had given his father this description of a group of holiday-makers who had sheltered from a thunderstorm under the porch of the Watkins home. The various alphabets show an increasing interest in this form of verse, following a correspondence with Eric Partridge, the doyen of comic alphabets.

The **Two Composers** limericks were written to taunt an opera-mad friend; the **German Romantics** as a mnemonic for an examination in German Literature. **Six Forms of Arrival** was written in response to a student who claimed that every poem held within itself its one and only possible form. It also commemorated the disastrous arrival in Seattle of his family, who found no-one waiting to meet them, because Vernon had confused the date.

All the poems in this book show that there was nothing in life, comic or serious, which Vernon Watkins could not turn into verse. We hope that readers will find as much enjoyment as Vernon did in writing them.

Gwen Watkins

This book is dedicated to the memory of Tristan Watkins.

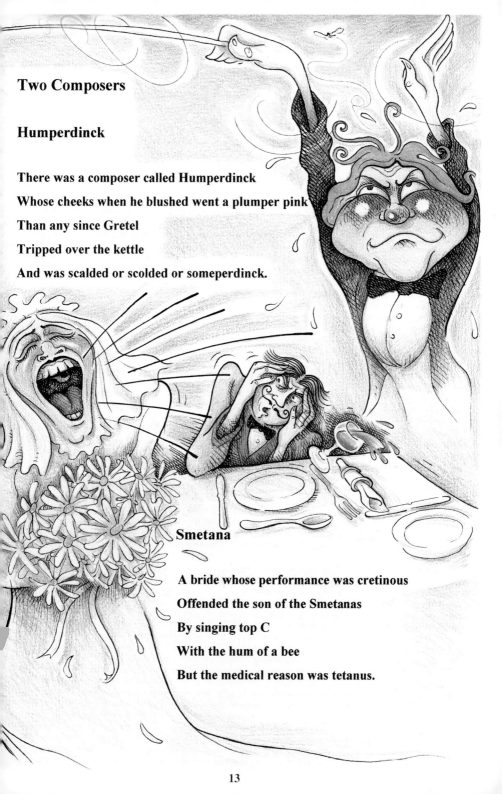

Two Composers

Humperdinck

There was a composer called Humperdinck
Whose cheeks when he blushed went a plumper pink
Than any since Gretel
Tripped over the kettle
And was scalded or scolded or someperdinck.

Smetana

A bride whose performance was cretinous
Offended the son of the Smetanas
By singing top C
With the hum of a bee
But the medical reason was tetanus.

An L M N T R E Alphabet

A was an angry Artist who always answered *'A?'*

B was a buzzing Bumble: where can that Bumble *B*?

C was a sinister Centipede with legs too quick to *C*.

D was a dear Dalmation Dog who dived in the river *D*.

E was an Eel: you could draw it on an easel easil *E*.

F was a flat and a floppy Fish who floundered, dumb and d *F*.

G was a Gull who gobbled the Fish, for it gave him ener *G*.

H was a huge Hyaena whose hunger none could assu *H*.

I was an Ibis who felt ill; you could tell he was ill by his *I*.

J was a nib to fit in a quill; you could get that quill from a *J*.

K was a kangaroo whose pouch was proof against de *K*.

L was a lazy little girl who laughed and said 'I'll t *L*!'

M was a Moor where magpies came, till a shotgun frightened *M*.

N was a nest the Magpies made; the eggs were laid by the *N*.

O was an Ogre counting up the coins that old men *O*.

P was the Picture we went to see, but first we had to *Q*.

R is for you, Remember, for I know who you *R*.

S is for Someone's solemn face; you or your brother can g *S*.

T is the time to see him, for he's very fond of *T*.

U is the ungry Unters, and one of the unters is *U*.

V is a venomous Viper; you can tell his head by the *V*.

W is a wise Wedding that will double you when you're *W*ed.

X cellent things shall follow, if you do as *Y* se men *Z*.

15

True Bearings 1.

Here nothing fits:
　Timbers have slits,
　　No thread on the screws,
　　The hatchet-head loose.
　　Fire-logs are knotted,
　　Sea-winds have rotted
　　The hinge of the gate.
　　One destitute grate
　　　Has dropped from its socket.
　　I had but to knock it
　　In clearing the chimney
　　For half an old brick
　　　And a slag-tip from Rhymney
　　　To tumble down quick.
The noise of soot falling,
The nest of a starling,
　I couldn't keep pace
　With the avalanche started
Till all the cold clinkers
The coal-man had carted
　Had dropped in my face.
　And in the grass plot,
　　That heaven for tinkers
　　Behind the back wall,
　　No saucepan or pot
　　Or basin or bowl
　　But has a big hole
　　　Where the water runs out.
There nettles grow tall
And buttercups sprout.
Saucers cracked wider
Than webs of a spider
Are lost in long grass
By a path where I pass
　To the shed that is rocking
　With iron shards knocking;
　In its floor-boards ferns root
　And the old water-shoot
　　Has slipped from its bracket.
　All night there's a racket
　Like a dog with a goose
　　Of the door that flies loose.

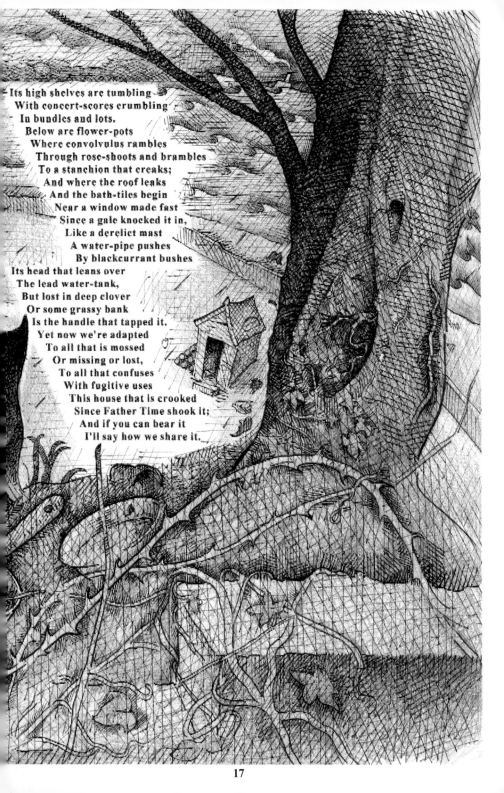

Its high shelves are tumbling
With concert-scores crumbling
In bundles and lots.
Below are flower-pots
Where convolvulus rambles
Through rose-shoots and brambles
To a stanchion that creaks;
And where the roof leaks
And the bath-tiles begin
Near a window made fast
Since a gale knocked it in,
Like a derelict mast
A water-pipe pushes
By blackcurrant bushes
Its head that leans over
The lead water-tank,
But lost in deep clover
Or some grassy bank
Is the handle that tapped it.
Yet now we're adapted
To all that is mossed
Or missing or lost,
To all that confuses
With fugitive uses
This house that is crooked
Since Father Time shook it;
And if you can bear it
I'll say how we share it.

Here everything fits
Here the tom-tits
Tap at each pane
Again and again
For crumbs on the plate
When breakfast is late
Then icicle weather
Holds all things together
We share rug and shawl
The rooms and the hall
Contract and grow harder
With frost, while the larder
Is locked against mice
Creeping in with the ice.

Then ponies half frozen
Surprise our long dozing.
We stare through the glass
At sheaves of white grass.
If the pine-logs are finished
Our stock is replenished
By a sea-gully good
That's littered with wood.
All Winter I fetch it
To chop with the hatchet
Coals light as be burn it
And poke it and turn it
And keep the door felted
While butter is melted

No heat must be lost
As the white bread we toast
Then, when all is ready,
The shimmer unsteady
On plate, knife or cup
Throws the first sunbeam up
To dance on the ceiling,
Sharp sunrise revealing
In shadow the string
The greedy tits cling
As they grip the fat plunder
Their talons swing under,
Each bird in succession
Regaining possession.

When the sun gains in power
Leaf opens, and flower
No rift or projection
Then seems imperfection,
No bracket or brace
No perch out of place
But all yield their inches
To robins and finches
Each fine thread of hair.
Like a feather shines fair.
The buckets with holes
Make neat shallow bowls;
The blackbird preens wings
Where the water-pipe flings

Its shade in the butt.
Whether open or shut,
This house is made richer
By every cracked pitcher,
By all that ran out
Through the long water-spout,
How tell the amount in
Which each is in debt?
We live by the fountain
That first made us wet.
Had the house not been tilted
When Father Time spilt it,
What plummet true-flighted
Had taught us to right it?

Eclogue

(to Berry)

Said the late express from Perth
As it ran into a buffer:
'Pray tell me, why on earth
Are engine wheels not tougher?'

Buffer: 'It's far too late to say.
The wheels are made much cheaper
Than they made them in my day.
You'd better ask the sleeper.'

Friend: 'I'll run along the kerb
Before the trucks are coupled.'

Telephone: 'There's no reply from Herb.
I'm sorry you've been troubled.'

Express: 'There must be someone near
To mend me. Life is hard if
There's not an engineer
Between this place and Cardiff.

Passed fit for children's greed,
Then broken, three days older.
For such alife you need
The patience of a solder.'

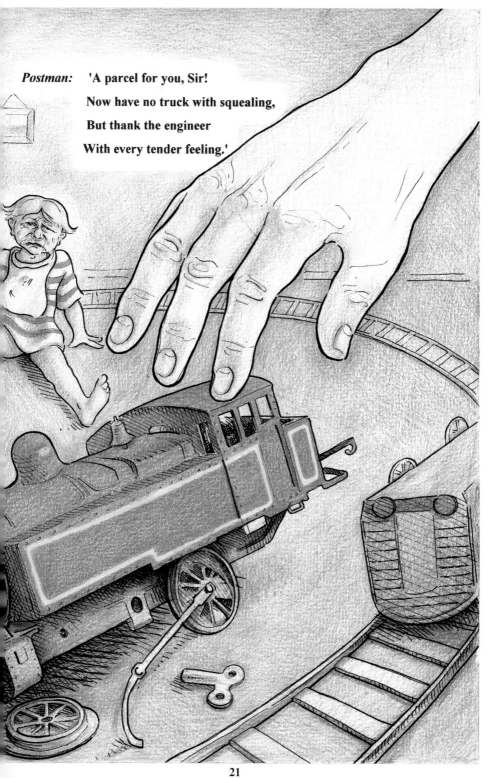

Six Forms of Arrival

1. I arrived in Seattle on Saturday, just after five.
   There was nobody waiting to meet me; the world became flat.
   There were people all buzzing about me like bees in a hive;
   It was hard to remember my luggage, the hold-all and hat.

2. After the bilious Atlantic, with baggage tossed in the hold,
   What excuse could there be? Either the train was late
   Or he was arriving with money, and somebody knocked him cold.
   Shame, shame, Seattle, unworthy of Washington State.

3. This was Seattle: I stepped from the train, prepared
   To grasp a professor's hand, then jump in his car.
   Three thousand miles of rehearsal, and now at last I was spared
   All but the knowledge that I had come so far.

4. At the station I sought from Seattle
   A professor with war-drum and rattle.
   Disappointment was grim;
   It was lucky for him
   He arrived there just after the battle.

5. Seattle, on Saturday. Thousands, and then nobody;
   Porter on porter, carrying away
   Luggage on the trolleys. Nobody I recognized

Waiting in the offing for my ten-week stay.

6. Seattle, have you no manners? Don't you recognize a
Syllabic poet when you see one? I took the *Daily
Chick* when I was a boy, lisped in hyphens; now I make them.
Even the steam hisses a stress at the end of the line.

Arrival in East Shelby

Never there was, nor ever shall be,
A better district than East Shelby,
Worthy of Whitman or of Emily,
To house my thoughts and books, and family.

Since Oscar mounted first the podium,
And pedants wrote a new Concordium
Of Dickens, fresh from Martin Chuzzlewit,
Food was laid on, for such to guzzle it.

Since Byron, sick of climbing Sunium,
Brought his baboons to the Wilsonian
And Auden, paying Clio homage,
Asked his hotelier, 'What's the damage?',

Poets by train or coach or hansom,
As the crow flies, or John Crowe Ransom,
Have come with sense, if not with money,
To look for breakfast in the Meany.

But what a stir and what a rumpus
Ran from the station round the Campus
When Thomas, finger stuck in bottle,
Taxi'd to Roethke in Seattle!

'Dear God,' I softly pray, as one does

Who fears the crash of balls through windows,

'May, now that Storm is propped with Morike,

Cricket appease North West America'.

Silly Old Bottly

Gareth and Rhiannon
Both have a plan on
Foot to recapture
Bottly of rapture.
Both are most cunning,
Here they come running,
Fighting and tumbling,
Playing and grumbling.
Tristan is near them
Truly I fear them.
Tacklings I beat off
I'll pull the teat off.
Slowly I squeeze it,
Quickly they seize it,
Why should they take it?
Angry and naked,
I pursue hotly
Silly old bottly.

Homage from Clio

Why not an epigrapH,
You from IschiA
Sailing to XanadU?
Tell poets in OxforD:
Ancient until it bE,
Never shall man be new, nor right, nor worthy of meN

Limitations

Rewrite the poets if you wilL;
Only allow them to gO
Back with tracks in snoW
Easily traceablE:
Reindeer which men kilL
Teach the limits of skilL.

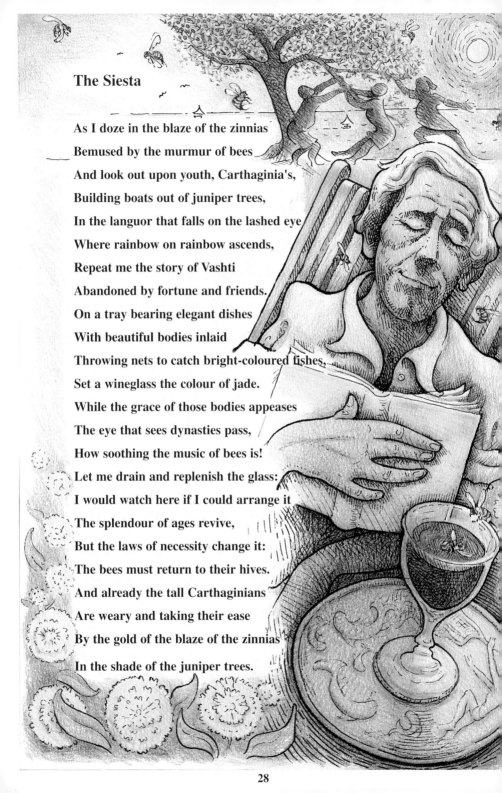

The Siesta

As I doze in the blaze of the zinnias
Bemused by the murmur of bees
And look out upon youth, Carthaginia's,
Building boats out of juniper trees,
In the languor that falls on the lashed eye
Where rainbow on rainbow ascends,
Repeat me the story of Vashti
Abandoned by fortune and friends.
On a tray bearing elegant dishes
With beautiful bodies inlaid
Throwing nets to catch bright-coloured fishes,
Set a wineglass the colour of jade.
While the grace of those bodies appeases
The eye that sees dynasties pass,
How soothing the music of bees is!
Let me drain and replenish the glass:
I would watch here if I could arrange it
The splendour of ages revive,
But the laws of necessity change it:
The bees must return to their hives.
And already the tall Carthaginians
Are weary and taking their ease
By the gold of the blaze of the zinnias
In the shade of the juniper trees.

Questions

1.

If the poet William Blake is right
And energy is eternal delight,
Why do their works compel us so
Whose delight and energy brought them woe?

2.

When Kierkegaard in judgment sits
On the strength of ultimate human ties,
Is not each culprit whom the cap fits
As near to the truth as he to lies?

3.

Fargue (Leon-Paul)
Thought love was the whole,
And why should I argue
With Leon-Paul Fargue?

4.

When Marcus Pimp extolled some verse
Who never had set eyes on worse,
What made his eulogy expire?
The ghost of Landor struck the liar.

Although little birds are much smaller than men
Our biggest cathedral was built by a Wren.

It is hard to portray extinct birds in a flock
But surely not one is as hard as a Roc

Don't Let's Hit the Moon

Don't let's hit the moon.
The moon is very sad.
Such a life it's had
Without its little spoon
Going round and round
And that little spoon
Nowhere to be found.

The moon is out of sorts.
I have begun to feel
It's rather down at heel.
No connoisseur of sports
It does not want a keel
But a little wheel
Going round and round
To enter all the ports
And that little wheel
Nowhere to be found.

If only we could throw
A little mistletoe
Or a little holly
To soothe its melancholy
Then it might be jolly

And some pleasure know
Going round and round
Like a little O
Lifted off the ground.

See how sad it looks.
Though the spoon was lost
In a night of frost
It can smell the soup
Made by all the cooks.
It can hear the gong.
Since it cannot eat
All it wants is feet
And a little hoop
Going round and round
Just to push along
But it cannot stoop
Ever to the ground.

The Musical Chairman

(on the occasion of Sir Oliver Franks leaving the Board)

What a loss, what a loss to the Banks,

What confusion in Stock Exchange ranks,

Now the sum of his knowledge

Has gone to a college

Whose marks must be turned into Franks.

The Stamp Collector

How rare the stamps of Martinique:
Their value I forget.
I have the cinq, I have the six,
I wish I had the set.

The Hoover

The Hoover is snorting,
Buzzing and shorting,
Booming and zooming
It snores to the rag:
There's plenty of room in
My beautiful bag.'
'Here it comes, here it comes,'
Says the dust to the crumbs;
Let's hide here together
And watch the white feather
Fly up and be swallowed,
By other things followed,
But never by us.'
'What a fuss, what a fuss,'
Says the hoover and hums:
'What dust! And what crumbs!
I must hum now my loudest
And longest and proudest
To get these crumbs in.
What a din, what a din;
And I hope that all boys
Run away from my noise
As I pick up the dust
And the crumbs and the crust,

The wool and the hair
Under table and chair,
Till I finish. Then I,
With a satisfied sigh,
Easy-going, grey-rubbered,
Contented and bright,
After work long begun
And finally done,
Retire to my cupboard
to sleep through the night.

The Channel Swimmer

Spurred by the Captain's life, from Dover's wall
He swung for France, persisting with a crawl
Worthy to make new history, but the ebb
Returned him, like a spider, to his Webb.

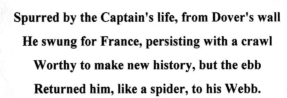

Cats

(translated from Theodor Storm)

Last year on Mayday morning my cat brought
Into the world six darling little kittens,
May-kittens, all pure white with black tail-tippings.
Indeed, it was a most enchanting childbed.
The cook, however, - cooks are savage beings,
And human kindness grows not in a kitchen -
Five of the six she meant to take and drown them,
Five white, with black tail-tippings, Mayday kittens
This monstrous woman had marked down to kill.
I took her down a peg. May heaven bless
Me for my human feeling. The dear kittens
They grew and grew, and in a short while ventured
To walk with high tails over hearth and courtyard;
Yes, as the cook, too, noticed with resentment,
They grew and grew, and nightly at her window
They tested out their darling little voices.
But I, however, as I watched them growing,
I prized myself and my humanity.

A year is round, and they are cats, those kittens,
And it is Mayday! - How can I describe it,
The scene that now enacts itself before me?
My whole house, from the cellar to the gable,

Its every corner is a childbed!
Here one is lying, there another kitten,
In cupboards, baskets, under stairs and table;
The old one even - no, I dare not say it,
Lies in the cook's own bed of maiden virtue!
And each, yes, each one of the seven she-cats
Has seven - think! - has seven youthful kittens,
May-kittens, all pure white with black tail-tippings!
The cook is raving; I can set no bounds
To the blind anger of this dreadful female.
She will go out and drown all nine-and-forty!
But I myself, - my head recoils from it:
O human kindness, how can I preserve you?
How can I start with six-and-fifty cats?

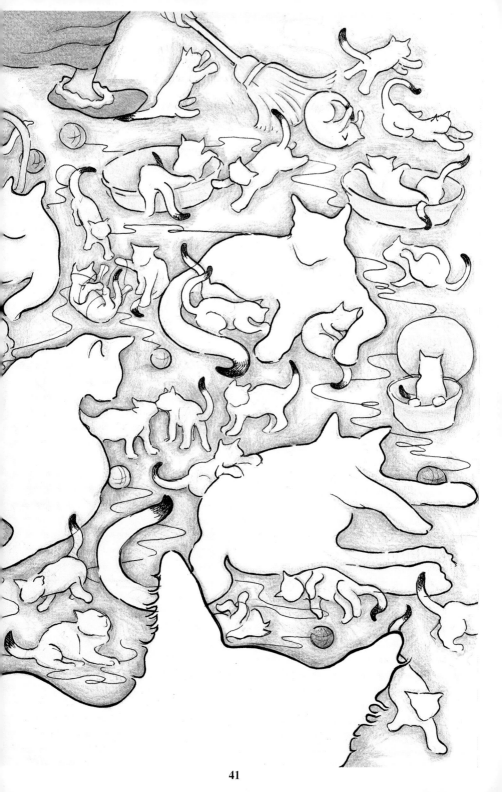

Aristophanes

You in the ring of fallen trees,
Buried Aristophanes,
Listen, as Doctor Klemperer hacks:
'Brek-kek-kek-kek- O axe, O axe!'

You were the knowledge-nuts' best seller;
You cracked them, like a truthful feller.
Against the bark of false esteem
You struck, and kept the axe-edge clean.
Best comedian, from the tomb
Your anger makes the right fruit come;
And he plays truest who can play
The music in its maker's way.

You've this in common, you and he:
You from the kernel know the tree.

Aristophanes

Tall in the ring of fallen trees,
Berried Aristophanes,
Make answer while the woodman hacks:
Break, ache, ache, ache - O axe, O axe!

The nuts of knowledge lack a sheller.
You cracked them, like a truthful feller.
Strong against clamberers you stood
And struck, but not as Henry would.

Sacked but for truth, inscribe this tomb:
'Level with liars I am come.
No beech am, yet to prove me hearty,
Shoot my last bolt, and cry 'Pro Arte':

Strength looks to heaven. The rest, I see,
Saw the wrong way. The oak's on me.'

The Museum

In the museum chambers I have seen
Amazing birds glitter behind the glass;
Strange butterflies astonish all who pass,
Streaked with vermilion, purple, gold and green.
The mighty elephant, with widespread ears,
Stands near the doorway, threatening all who climb
Up the stone staircase, worn by the tread of Time,
To view dead monsters. Man no longer fears
His ancient fury, - people now go by
Vaguely amused at this gigantic corpse,
His tusks, which Time eventually warps,
And the dull frozen fire in his eye.
They see the wolves in their transparent cage,
The kingly lion, with his yellow mane,
Whose fierce teeth are a tale of wrath and pain,
Though his loud roar has long been dulled by age.
There lies the tiger - golden-striped and black,
There the dark panther poised for sudden spring,
And there the leopard crouches, listening
For the departed prey, that ne'er come back;
And in the upper rooms enormous bones,
Which moved a hundred thousand years ago,
Play their strange parts in this ironic show,
Whose principal actors are gaunt skeletons.

Welcome to Causley

As soon as we heard

Our Chairman had stirred

The Launceston poet,

We let the folk know it.

Though some looked askance

From Looe to Penzance,

The news travelled faster

From master to master,

And they had no scruples

In rounding up pupils

From Bodmin to Borstal

To come to St. Austell

And leave all their homework,

Brushwork and comb-work,

Like husbands and wives

Who start from St. Ives

Before Barbara Hepworth

Has finished a shape worth

Some figure terrific

And stopped all the traffic

To let it be shipped

In the hold like a crypt

Of the latest Queen liner,

A bull among china

Or ship in a bottle.

And let Aristotle

Allow us to quote

What he muttered or wrote

When he felt himself harassed

Or bored or embarrassed

By learning too pompous

And wanted a rumpus:

'In this and each age

To think like a sage

But speak like the folk

Is the mark of true work.'

This saying, demanding

Such rare understanding,

Too often neglected

And seldom expected,

How well you obey it,

Adapt and display it,

In all that you write.

We, therefore, delight

To hear you, regretting

No more to this meeting

Were able to come.

And yet, if the sum

Of hearers were stated

Since song was created

Or lyric begun,

Though many transfigure

The form of that figure,

It cannot grow bigger:

The number is One.

The Older Child's Larder Alphabet

A was Ann:
B was But
Can, can
the Door be shut?
E was Extra
Fine to Fit.
'Go, go
and Hammer it!'
I was I:
J was Jim.
'Keep, keep
a Look for him!'
M was Mince
N was Nice,
O, O,
the Pastry Pies!
Q was Quiet:
'R you in?'
See, see
the Toffee Tin!
U an Uproar
Vandals vowed
Was, was
Xtremely loud.
Yes! Beat it, or you'll be

Zoomed upon by **Zebedee!**

A Survey of the German Romantic Movement

The Critique of Pure Reason
Announced the new season
Which first Bishop Berkeley
Saw through a glass darkly.

Goethe
Was a terrible flirter.
'He started at nine,'
Said Charlotte von Stein.

For an act of sheer patience
In long conversations
When boredom might wreck a man,
I hand it to Eckermann.

Schopenhauer
Used eloquent power
To explain to the nosey
That life isn't cosy.

Heine was quicker
Than any old sticker
Born East of that river
So bad for his liver.

Lessing

Was so slow at dressing,

You could travel to Hants

While he put on his pants.

Yet he, when it came

To the epigram game

Or the Parthian shot,

Gave as good as he got.

First, Beethoven's power;

Then Holderlin's Tower:

Both eager to quicken,

But the poet was stricken.

Tieck,

If he wanted to speak

To a man without malice,

Would call on Novalis.

Seeing Germany fighting

With France for the Rhine,

'Hands off!' cried Heine,

'That river is mine!'

Schiller

Grew iller and iller

Till in eighteen-five

He wasn't alive.

Uhland

Was no fuhl, and

Nietzsche

No tietzsche.

But, in spite of their antics,

The German Romantics

In metrical noise

Were well-behaved boys.

Rain

Pooly, drippy people
On a pooly, drippy day
Were looking for a little house
And couldn't find the way.

They all had their umbrellas up,
And bumped into each other,
A little girl, a little boy,
Their father and their mother.

The reason for their wandering
And their extreme distress
Would not exist if they had known
The name or the address.

The little girl said 'There it is!'
The boy said 'No, it isn't!'
And so by stages they arrived
At 30 Dolphin Crescent.

And there a man stood waiting
With a fierce, indignant look
And a fierce, indignant spaniel
And a fierce, indignant book.

And he said, 'If you've lost your way
And want a cup of tea,
Be certain I can fix you up
In Canto Twenty-Three.'

So then he gave them food and drink
But still they asked for more.
The boy said, 'What we want, I think,
Is Canto Twenty-Four.'

His mother said, 'Down, little dog!'
'How can you be so silly?'
And turning to the gentleman,
'You must excuse our Willy.'

We cannot always find our way
Nor always where to go,
But how to settle there, they say,
Is something we should know.

Hairy Beary

'Hairy Beary, where is he,
On the land or on the sea?'
'Is he brown or is he black?'
'He's the white one in the pack.'

Verses for Two Children

1.

Remember this:
Hid is heaven
In all true bliss.
All was given,
Now in moments,
Now in years,
Once, for your joy's
New-sprung tears

2.

God may translate
All to praise.
Reason with fate
Equal weighs
Till power, confessing,
Holds the right blessing.

For a Golden Wedding

Now for fifty years your slave,
All you took I gladly gave.
On the day you find me thrifty
Touch me for another fifty

XXX

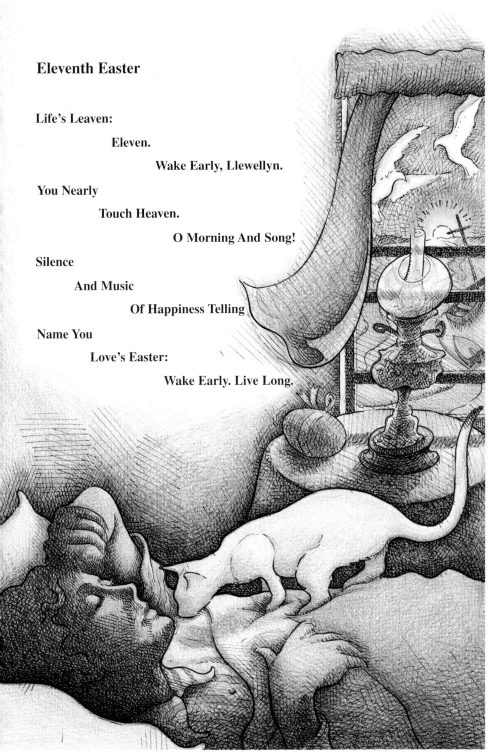

Eleventh Easter

Life's Leaven:

        Eleven.

            Wake Early, Llewellyn.

You Nearly

        Touch Heaven.

            O Morning And Song!

Silence

        And Music

            Of Happiness Telling

Name You

        Love's Easter:

            Wake Early. Live Long.

The Spider's Killen Da

A spider span
A thread in *Jan*.
In early *Feb*
She made a web.
She stretched it far
To middle *Mar*
Then tried to drape
A branch in *Ap*
But winds of *May*
Blew all away.
She hid, but soon
In early *Jun*
She took her spool
And all through *Jul*
Right on to *Aug*
She made a morgue.
Her bridegroom leapt
To her in *Sept*
But him she knocked
For six in *Oct*.
So then she wove
A web in *Nov*
Inscribed in *Dec*
With 'REST IN PEACE.'

60

Epilogue

63